A WEST HAM LIFE:

Parents' Centre Publications

1984

Published as Parents' Centre Publication No. 36
by Newham Parents' Centre, 747 Barking Road, London E13 9ER.

© Newham Parents Centre and William Perry.

ISBN 0 906985 02 1

Printed by the Moffat Group of Companies

The illustrations appear by kind permission of:
William George Perry, cover.
The London Borough of Newham Library Service,
The Passmore Edwards Museum, Stratford,
The City of London, Guildhall,
Charrington Breweries Ltd.,
Line drawings by John Mitchell and Paul Cockburn.

THE NEWHAM PARENTS' CENTRE GRATEFULLY ACKNOWLEDGES THE
FINANCIAL ASSISTANCE OF THE GREATER LONDON ARTS ASSOCIATION AND
THE BRITISH LIBRARY, TOWARDS THE COSTS OF THE PUBLISHING AND
RESEARCH WORK UNDERTAKEN BY THE CENTRE.

This publication is humbly dedicated to Mr. Perry's mother and father.

IV

INTRODUCTION

Parents' Centre Publications are one feature of the activities of the Newham Parents' Centre. The Centre is a registered charity of residents and workers in the London Borough of Newham, committed to the improvement of local education, both institutional and cultural.

During the last seven years, the Centre has produced regular newsletters and information booklets, and these have been distributed through a network of local contacts. In 1979, a natural development of this work was the establishment of a community publishing project with the aim of encouraging and promoting local authorship and books of local interest. "A West Ham Life: William George Perry" is the third such feature publication, and the first in a series of local biographies which will help preserve some aspects of the unique nature of life in East London.

The production of this book owes a great debt to Mr. Ken Madgett, of North East London Polytechnic, who first brought the recollections of Mr. Perry to the attention of the Centre. Further acknowledgement must be made of the considerable efforts of Philip Wainwright, without whom, this book would have taken even longer to produce! The efforts of those members of diverse institutions who helped trace the illustrations are also gratefully noted.

This book evolved from taped conversations with Mr. Perry on seperate occasions since 1980. As such, the publishers wish to point out that in keeping with the tradition of oral history that this book represents, efforts have been made to avoid altering the way Mr. Perry would have told the stories to a listener. This style might not be to everyone's taste, but it is a truer record of one man's memory.

PAUL COCKBURN

CONTENTS

Home

I was born in Hancock Road, Bromley-by-Bow on November 4th, 1891.

At age of four I was moved to the posh end of Caistor Park Road, that was the Park end. My father went to work at Three Mills Distillery, Bow. I just remember going into a lovely, redbrick house, near West Ham Park.

My father came home one day. I was around six or seven years old, roughly — I may have been older, I may have been younger, I don't know — but I heard him say to my mother:

"I've got the sack."

"Oh," she said, "Well, we'll have to find something else."

"Oh", he said. "Don't worry about that," he said, "I've got something in mind."

We moved from Caistor Park Road because my father, at the age of 40 years, was reckoned to be too old to be at work at the distillery.

There were seven of us in the family. I can remember my mother and father going out, and my three sisters looking after me and my brother. They went to look at a house at 39 Lucas Road, Abbey Lane, Stratford. It was a rotten hole, absolutely rotten. I can remember the van coming round, packing up the furniture at Caistor Park Road, and moving us to Abbey Lane. When we got there, there was no glass in the window spaces and bugs were climbing up and down the walls, but what my father wanted was the yard, a backyard with plenty of sheds. We rented the house for 6s 6d per week.

Living in Abbey Lane, we were a very, very close community, the people knew each other, and the Perry family was well known. Now, in the "Lane", there was one public house which was open all day long, and the women used to get their dinner all ready by peeling the potatoes and doing the greens whilst in the pub over half a pint of beer.

1

They used to have a game down Abbey Lane. 'Cause down Abbey Lane, they had the railings coming down to part the two doors of houses, and they had big knockers on the doors. So, they'd get a lump of rope, tie this on the knocker and on the railings, knock the door and run away. When people tried to open the doors, they couldn't open them. There were other games. They used to call one: "I've seen the knacker; one, two, three." You'd have a milk tin — there was no milk like we have it today, we always had condensed milk — so you used to get an empty milk tin, and there'd be about six or eight people, boys or girls, playing, and you'd throw the tin, and the boy would have to go and pick the tin up in the road, walk backwards, and he'd have to find people hiding in the houses. There was that game.

But I never played much. Those days, there was nothing. Children hadn't got any bread and butter, and children were very, very poor. Thank God I was never. We were never poor. But a lot of children were. They used to go at the back of the stalls along Stratford High Street, and pick up specked apples, or specked oranges, or whatever — and eat them, because they were hungry.

Working With My Father

Lucas Road was a cul-de-sac, and my father wanted the yard for his business. And for that, he got a handbarrow, and he paid a shilling a week on hire for this handbarrow, and he pulled it round the streets selling firewood, and I used to go out there. I used to help him chop up the wood and carry it. I can remember him going to Romford Market, and buying up a donkey. I can remember the auctioneer being in like a triangle wall, with a pulpit going round, selling the donkeys and ponies, and he bought this donkey, and walked all the way from Romford Market to Stratford. Little did I know that I was going there in another month's time, and this time he was going to buy a pony.

I think my father paid 15s for the donkey, and I think he paid 30s for the pony.

On the way back, I can remember my father saying to me:

"Look after this pony."

He was driving a donkey and cart, and it had got so late that we had to have a light on the donkey-barrow. He went into a shop and he bought a paper lantern or "chinese lantern", and put it on the rail of the barrow. Going along, with the wind and swaying of the barrow, the paper caught light with the candle. A copper pulled him up, and there was just the wire handle on the rail of the barrow and my father said:

"There you are, it's just burnt."

"Doesn't matter."

The policeman locked him up, and he was fined 10s or seven days for having no light on the barrow. He paid the ten bob.

When he got the pony home, he said to my brother, he said:

"Let's put him in the shafts and see what he can do," and I can always remember this. The pony wouldn't budge, he would not pull at all. So he says:

3

"Alright," he says, "Go back in the yard and get a little wisp of hay, and put it underneath his belly," he says, "and as I get up into the barrow, set light to that hay, and see if he'll pull then." As the hay flared up and the pony felt the heat, you know, on his tummy, he didn't jib any more. He cured that pony of jibbing.

My father was very well known in Stratford. There used to be a sweet stall, and this man used to make his own toffee over a coke fire. He used to buy coke off my father, and used to have the sugar and what have you. His stall was right opposite a street called Chapel Street. As my father was going past Chapel Street, a lump of paper flew out of the street, right across the top of the pony's face, and it shied with it right into this bloke's stall. Funny thing, it shied into his stall, and knocked his fire all over, his toffee all over, oh crumbs, it did make a mess. But, being pals like, my father and this man, he never pressed charges or anything like that.

My father built his business, which comprised of firewood and coke, and at Christmastide, he would go to the Stratford Market and buy three or four boxes of oranges which he sold for 48 oranges for one shilling, and if you bought one shilling's worth you would get two extra, making 50 oranges. And that was the day when he said to me:

"Now you are 10 years old, it's nearly time you learned to stand on your own two feet and start selling."

He gave me a donkey and a barrow to look after, and I was sent out with two sacks of firewood and the well of the barrow loaded with loose wood. I sold the wood for 1d a basket, the basket was about 6" high and 9" across; 1d a basket or three baskets for 2½d. I built up a round around the Leytonstone Road, and there was a man there I remember. When I went there he used to buy a sack of wood for half a crown, and that took a load of weight off the donkey. I used to meet my father when I was nearly sold out, at a public house in Plashet Road which had a huge trough in front of the pub. If he got there first, he would wait for me, and if I got there first I would wait for him. He would have his drop of beer and nearly always it was cold weather and wintertime, and I would have a glass of peppermint and he would have his half pint of beer for 1d, and my peppermint was also 1d.

I would go across the road to a little chandler's shop and buy a ha'peth of broken biscuits, and we used to come home — he would take the lead and I would follow. When I got home I would empty my pockets of the money I had taken.

My father, he had a pony and trolley and I had a donkey and barrow. He would go to the West Ham Coke Company and buy a half-chaldron of coke which the pony used to drag along and I would have a big bag on the barrow and we would take the coke home. We would sell the coke again, a pailful for a penny and if you wanted three pails, that would also be 2½d.

We had no gas in those days and people had light by paraffin oil, and I can remember when people had candles.

To tell you the truth, naturally my father with his business there was a lot of horse manure — we used to call it dung. Around West Ham was the Pumping Station; alongside of the Pumping Station there was about four or five houses. The people in those houses were given an allotment right alongside their houses almost, but the allotments were all together and the houses were all together. My father would say to me when I came home from school at 4 pm:

"Load up that donkey barrow and take a load of dung round on the allotments." I never had the keys to get in the gate, but I used to have to pull the donkey right near the railings and get the fork and put the manure over the fence. After emptying the barrow which was very, very heavy, and I was not very tall or big, and only 11-12 years of age, I would knock at the door and tell the man that I had put the dung over the fence. He would say:

"Thank you very much," and he would give me a penny, and when you come to think of it, a farthing's worth of sweets was not too bad. But then, I think it was worth more than one penny to push the manure over the railings — it was very hard work.

Mother and Father

My father could not read or write, but my mother was well educated, and my uncle was a lawyer. My father had a lot of barrows which the people used to pull along, also donkey barrows and vans, and he wanted to put on the side of the barrow the name and address and "On Hire". We had plenty of coke, and a big pail with holes in, and a sharp poker. Mother would line out the name, "Robert Perry, 39 Lucas Road, Stratford, On Hire," and she would put that out in chalk, and he would put the red hot poker to put on his name and address, and "On Hire".

My mother had paid tuppence a week to go to school. She lived in Rochford, near Southend, and her father must have been a very wealthy man, because he sent her to school, and he sent her brother to school. That was why my mother was so bent on sending me to school, because my brother got his living as an iron moulder, and my sisters, they all married. One was married to a sailor; one was married to a matchworker, he used to make matches at Bell's match factory; another one was working at the iron foundry; another one was working at Harris and Barbers, the horse slaughterers — that was my oldest sister; and the other one worked at the jute, down Wharf Road. She wore clogs. Life was so different those days, you'd hardly know it. Go out years ago, and you used to find people playing what they call hopscotch. They'd chalk on the pavement, wouldn't they, different numbers, and you've got to get your feet in — I think that's right.

My mother really married beneath her. To marry a bloke who couldn't read nor write. It was really common in those days, people who couldn't read nor write, there was no free schooling.

My father retired at the age of about 69 to 70 years. There was no old age pension in those days, and he went to live in Durham Road, Canning Town. In 1910 or 1911, I put him in for the old age pension 5s a week. He didn't want it, as he was a very reserved man, and as I have said before, he could not read or write, and I put him in, but he didn't know anything about it, and I wrote his name, and he put his cross there and he got his pension of 5s a week.

From there, after about 5 years, I got married in 1917 and we lived at Middle Road, right near my mother, after my father passed away in 1916. My father was 78 when he died, and he died of senile decay, and he gradually faded away. My mother died in 1923.

7

Blind Ben

In Lucas Road, where I lived, there was a man who was blind and his name was Blind Ben.

I never hardly played in the street, but the blind man would like me to go with him about 6.30-7.30 in the evening, and play a portable harmonium outside pubs. I would lead him there and I always remember that wild birds were allowed to be caught in those days, and he used to love to catch linnets. He had a linnet, and we used to take it to the pub, opposite Carpenter's Road, called "The Carpenter's Arms". We would sit under a shelf, and he would put the linnet on the shelf, and although he was blind, he had good hearing, and he would say to me:

"There you are, here he goes, here he goes, he is singing again," and I would get up and I would see the little bird's throat wobbling as it sang.

We would come out of the pub and we would go home. There were prizes for the bird singing; 2/6d first prize, 2/- second prize and 1/-for the third prize.

He got these birds himself in the Shute near Abbey Lane, getting them in a net, greenfinches as well as linnets then. In the street again there was a man who was a cripple and he used to make wire baskets. He would have big coils of wire and he used to make these hanging baskets for conservatories. He used to sell the baskets for 1d and 2d each; he sold the wire baskets to the rich people of Forest Gate who had conservatories.

Recalling Blind Ben, I would like to say that nearly every public house we went to, after playing outside the public house with his portable harmonium, he would give me a little velvet bag with a bit of wire so that the bag kept open, and we would go to the customers in the pub and say:

"Pity the blind. Pity the blind" — nearly always he would put two half-pennies or two pennies in the bag so they would jingle, saying — "Pity the blind". He would always have his hand on my shoulder because I was not a very tall boy.

"We used a lot of public houses"

We used a lot of public houses. Those days there were different licensing hours; for the Stratford side of Bow Bridge the public houses used to close 11 o'clock, but over the Bow Bridge side they closed at 12 o'clock and we used to hurry over Bow Bridge and get to the public house that closed at 12 o'clock and sometimes I would not get home ready for school, not until about 12.30, but my mother did not mind because I was helping a blind man.

Old Blind Ben, he had a daughter, and I was very sweet on her, his daughter. My mother said to me, you don't want to get married to her; he's got bad eyesight, he's blind — you don't want to marry, in case it happens to her.

People were like that years ago, you know, they were, honestly. "Don't go in there . . ." But this old Blind Ben, he was very clever with his hands. He'd come and get a big coil of all strands of wire, this sixteenth of an inch thick wire, or thirty-second of an inch thick wire, very thin, and he'd make these hanging baskets.

School

I was ten years old and still at school.

At my school, they were very, very strict. You would have the bell rung, and people could hear it in their houses, they would hear the bell rung at a quarter to nine until ten to nine. Ten to nine it would go off till five to nine. Five to nine it would go on again till nine o'clock — that'd be the last bell. Then you were late. You were supposed to be at your desk ready for the teacher to come into the class, and if you were not there, you would have to have a good excuse why you were held up. If you were not there you would be registered as late and possibly get the cane. If I got there early for school, or anyone else, the Head Master would ask you to go into the lobby and ring the bell.

If there was something serious that you had done, the teacher would say:

"Get out!" and he would make you lean over the desk and wallop you on the backside with the cane, and that was that. Examples of naughtiness were if you hit a girl or jumped over the railings. We had an allotment near to the school and if an allotment holder found his produce had been damaged, he would want to know who had done this; and if some boy would tell on another that would be reckoned as serious; bad work and carlessness were punishable as well. If you were sent to the Headmaster, that was extra bad.

I went to Holbrook Road School, when we lived at Caistor Park Road. From Abbey Lane I went to school at the Three Mills School; from there my mother found me coming out from school going to buy an apple for the teacher.

"What are you doing?" she said.

"I am going to get an apple for Mr. Gibbons, the teacher," I said.

"I send you there to learn, not to go and run errands," she said. So she came to the Head Master and complained that her boy was buying apples for the teacher.

11

Work was hard to find, and you've got to remember I was fourteen years old, and you could leave school then at thirteen, if you wished; but my mother wouldn't let me leave school, because my father wasn't in a bad sort of a job.

My mother was always a one for schooling. Many a time, boys and girls would play truant. You'd have a School Board man come round in those days, and say:

"Your boy or your girl hasn't been to school today, why was it?" and of course the woman or the man would be surprised:

"Well, I sent him."

But I would nearly always be at school early.

We had reading, writing and arithmetic. That's all. But as I was leaving, we did start to have Euclid. I went to Toynbee Hall in Commercial Road for evening lessons after I left school. My mother and Tommy Bottley said:

"Why don't you go, you're a blooming good writer." And I was so.

I remember my Head Teacher, Mr Gayward, Mr Gibbons, Mr Forcett, that was in the big boys like — I don't remember when I was in the infants or anything like that. But — the boys were the boys and the girls were the girls, there wasn't any mixed schooling in those days.

Funerals

The ordinary person who died at home probably could not afford the funeral, so they would be buried by the Parish. The coffin would be an ordinary plain wooden coffin in a closed hearse. You could not see the coffin at all. The one black horse used to pull the hearse and the mourners would have to go to the cemetery either by tram or bus.

You could always tell whether the person was well off or not. If they were well off, the horses used to have big plumes on their heads, also black velvet sashes going down their bodies, and the men used to have high hats with black ribbon round. If it was a rich man's funeral it would be loaded with flowers, but if it was a poor funeral there would hardly be any floral tributes on the coffin.

A most interesting thing is when General Booth died, the City Corporation was responsible for the sanding out of the City from Eastcheap to Bishopsgate. In those days you had either wood blocks or asphalt roads, and people used to slip if the rain came down, so we put sand down so that people could get a good grip. General Booth was buried at Abney Park Cemetery, and the lads and lassies and lovely bands were playing and all singing and dancing; very, very joyful that he was going to a better place, or so they thought.

Donkeys

When I went to school, during my dinner time, my father would ask me to take a donkey to be shod. Abbey Lane then was parted off, a tollgate across the road. There was two old couples that used to live in the house that used to guard this tollgate. So I had to get the donkey through the tollgate. But my father would not pay the half-penny for the man to open the tollgate, so I had to push the donkey through. The tollgate was at the bottom of Abbey Lane and when you turned round to the left you had to pass the Mill, and further on you went to the Market Hill which was over Stratford Market.

There were several blacksmiths at West Ham. The one my father used to use was just past the Mills in Abbey Lane, and the man there, I don't know his real name, but he was called "Mo". Everything he used to say was "Half-a-mo".

The other blacksmiths were at Channelsea River in High Street, Stratford, and at Sugar House Lane in Stratford again.

When I was courting, I had to go across the Memorial Ground. It was very, very dark, and the moon would shine now and again. All of a sudden, I noticed in the distance there was something of a grey object moving, then stopping, then moving, then stopping — and it really frightened me. I said to myself:

"I have to go home!" It was about 1 o'clock in the morning. I got halfway across the Memorial Ground and it stopped again, and put its head up — what was it? It was a donkey eating the grass!

One thing I remember very clearly in my mind, is that my father liked his half-pint of beer every day and he used to use one public house, the Two Brewers Public House in Stratford High Street. He was in there one day — I was with him because children under the age of 14 were allowed to go into public houses at that time — and, I remember, that there was a man in there who bet my father that he would not make the donkey drunk. My father loved this particular donkey; in fact he used to let this donkey stray all around the yard, and we had a very, very big yard.

14

"The tollgate at the bottom of the Abbey Lane"

Well, let me tell you that my father took him on. In those days you had "four-ale", that means a quart of ale cost 4d, and there was another stronger drink which you could buy and that was called "old ale" which was around 8d per quart. Now, in the public house they used to have a glass barrel that had arrowroot biscuits in. These biscuits would measure around 5" across. So he got his biscuit which was bought for 1d, and he got half a pint of old ale. He took the ale out in a pewter pot to the donkey, which was standing outside in Stratford High Street, and took the bit out of its mouth so that it could eat the biscuit quite easily, and he soaked this biscuit in the old ale and gave it to the donkey.

The consequence was that he reckoned that the donkey drank a good three parts of the half-pint of old ale. So what did we do with the other part? My father was a dab hand at pulling at a horse or donkey's toungue at one side and just poured the remaining old ale down the donkey's throat.

We went back into the pub, thinking that everything was OK. The man said to my father:

"I told you you would not make the donkey drunk."

When we came out of the pub, the donkey was down on its two front knees, and the man said:

"Well, how are you going to get along now?" Remember, the donkey was in the shafts. We weighed on the back of the barrow and lifted the donkey up, and got the donkey back to the stable, and it was straggling all over the road. It was a good job that the RSPCA was not around in those days.

But, he really did get the donkey drunk, and afterwards, the donkey sort of looked forward every time my father went to the Two Brewers public house, and look around for its usual half-pint of old ale.

My father always looked after his cattle, his donkeys and his ponies. Every weekend, if they were not out on hire, they would have a hot bran mash.

Getting a Job

Work was very hard to get in those days. My mother had a boy-friend. This Mr Parker was a big noise for the Great Eastern Railway Printing Department, down the Burford Road. When I left the school, he said to my mother:

"Oh yes, I'll get Will a job," he said, "I'll get Will a job in the printing office." But on the GER those days, they wanted three references. Remember, I was fourteen years old. So I've got to find three references, one from the school, one from a tradesman and one from the vicar. We got one from the school — a very, very good one — and a good one from Mr Stone, the corner shop bloke. But the vicar would not give me one. I suppose, really, he was right, because my mother used to send me to Sunday School, but I never used to go. I should have gone to Christchurch, Stratford, with Mr Savanti as the vicar. I can see my mother now, she had this cape on and a bonnet with the spangles — you know, that glitter as you move your arm. Over the door, when we went into the vestry, there was a round lamp, and there was the gas jet burning over the nipple.

My mother said:

"Oh, I've brought my boy along for you to give him a reference. He's got a job at the Great Eastern Railway, at the printing offices."

And he looks at me — he was an elderly man, with a beard:

"I don't know that I've ever seen him much." The "much" made me laugh. To cut a long story short, I've got my arm underneath my mother's cape, holding her arm — I'm the little boy. At the finish, he's making such a bloody mouthful of it, I said to my mother:

"Come along, mother, I'm the fallen sheep, he is supposed to help me, but it seems that he doesn't want to". Little did he know that when I used to get to school early, Mr Gibbons used to say:

"Bible. Bible out!" and I used to read this to pass the time. And when I said this to that bloody vicar, he said:

"Get out! Get out!"

That was that. We came away from there, and of course I never got the job.

No, there wasn't much work.

My brother-in-law, he worked for Harris and Barbers, the horse slaughterers down Sugar House Lane, because horse meat was all the go — they used to have cats' meat from horses, but if it was a donkey, they didn't want donkey meat for cats. They used to have that for manure to put on the land. My brother used to fetch some kind of steak, or whatever you like to call it. It's very, very sweet, horse flesh, very sweet indeed.

He got out of work, and the West Ham Council, they inaugurated a scheme whereby they opened soup kitchens by the church. Poverty was very, very bad. You could go in there and buy a penny bowl of soup and take a bit of bread with you, and that was your dinner. And the West Ham Borough Council inaugurated the scheme where they dug the Hollow Pond in Wanstead. For half a crown a day, a bloke could go and dig out this Hollow Pond, but you could only do a day's work.

And I can remember in 1930, 1931, queues lining outside the gates in Stoney Lane Depot waiting for work to clear the snow, and I've had with me and Tommy Gosnall (the ganger up on Tower Bridge, Jimmy Gass used to love me to be the foreman), 9 men in the gang, excluding the ganger. And I'd have 20 odd men come up from Stoney Lane Depot, where they used to line up to get work for 1s 4d an hour, and they could only do 4 hours.

Over the south side of Tower Bridge, that's over the Bermondsey side, there was a coffee stall, and the poor devils, some of them — shifting snow for 1s 4d an hour — I can remember having hardly a bit of boot on their feet. I'd have two bob's worth of pennies in my pocket, and I'd say to Tommy:

"Him, him, him and him; send them out for tea this morning. There's tuppence for a penny bun and a penny cup of tea." And do you know, there was method in my madness. I found out that I got more work out of those men than what I did if I didn't give it to them. And nearly always, when Tommy Gosnall took those men back to get their pay, the 1s 4d an hour, that'd be 5s 4d for four hours, that odd fourpence came back to me, and Tommy Gosnall would say:

"Here you are Bill, here's your money back".

There was a man dived off the high level. He should have waited until the tide was high, but it was only half high. He dived off the high level, and stuck his head into the mud; and he killed himself.

Working for the City of London

I've been lucky in my life. Work was very hard to get, but I saw an old friend of mine — Tommy Bottley — who worked for the City of London Corporation. I'd already had one job, but the Stone Masons went broke.

"Why don't you come up, you might get a job."

So I went up on the Friday and got a job at 6s per week, to go out on the streets with shovel, broom and brush and pick up the paper and horse droppings. But luck was on my side. Mr Dudley, the man who was in the Depot, said to me:

"Write your name and address".

My mother had always said to me:

"You make your downstrokes thick, and if you make your downstrokes thick like that, you can always join them up and make letters." So I wrote my name and address.

"Hmm, alright," he said, "start away. Go over the road," he said, "and go into the coffee room, get your coffee". In those days, the boys was so hard up that the Corporation used to serve us coffee, and you used to take a couple of slices of bread and butter, and that was your breakfast. You used to start work at eight o'clock.

On this day I went out with the pan and brush, and on the following day, Tommy Bottley came to me, and he said:

"You're not going to go out any more," he said, "you've got to stop in here and see Mr Dudley."

And Mr Dudley said:

"Ah, you haven't gone out. Very good," he said, "Sit down there, and write your name and address again." So I wrote my name and address again.

"Now, I don't want you to go out anymore," he said, "You're going to be my office boy. The other boy what's been my office boy, Jimmy Eares, he's been with me for six years, and I'm hoping that you'll be with me for six years."

And do you know, that man pushed me. If anybody had a good father, he was a good father to me, he was really. He pushed me, wherever he was. I only went out the one day. I got six shillings a week for being an office boy; I'd have got six shillings a week if I'd gone out on the streets.

Time went on.

You didn't pass the doctor until you was twenty-one. That was really wrong, because a boy who didn't pass the doctor, he couldn't get a job when he was twenty-one, but he could get a job when he was sixteen or seventeen. We altered all that, as I got older, we altered all that . . .

When I came out of the office, Mr Dudley didn't want to lose me. So all I done was, make squeegees and scoops that the boys used to use. I got too old for that, and Tommy Bottley was getting a little bit ancient for storekeeping, so he retired and I went to the stores as a storekeeper. Then, Mr Parker, the Boys' Foreman, I think he died, and Mr Dudley said:

"Here you are — Boys' Foreman, come on," and I was made the Boys' Foreman of "B" Division.

You could always hear Mr Dudley's feet. You could always hear Mr Dudley coming down the lane, because he had a wooden leg, and it didn't bend at the knee. He used to swing his leg, and you could hear it go plonk, plonk, plonk. A very big man, he was, stout. He lost his leg through the van running over it.

When Mr Dudley died, it was Mrs Dudley's wish that I should go to his funeral; oh, a lovely old girl she was. And she said to Jimmy Lewis, who was smoking his meerschaum pipe:

"Jimmy," she said, "Put that pipe out. The smoke's getting in my curtains". I did miss Mr Dudley, I did really.

"A six shillings a week . . . to pick up paper and horses droppings"

In 1914 I joined up in Lord Kitchener's scheme; went into the army. I was in the stores 1914. We had to send stores out to all the lavatories, like what women wear, and soda and soap, nail brushes, scrubbing brushes, dusters and what have you. And I went straight back to my job; that was one of the conditions, if you went into the army. One thing I had to do, when I was over the toilets as well, I used to have to take the numbers down of the locks; because the attendants used to pay their money in to Upper Thames Street, and that man used to pay the money into the bank and take the book to the Guildhall. So every Monday, round about, say, half past eleven, twelve o'clock, I would go to the Guildhall and hand in my book of all the numbers of the toilets to see if the attendants were honest or not.

Anyway, then I got Men's Foreman, and stayed Men's Foreman until I retired in 1953. I didn't want to work anymore. I had a good pension. I paid 6d a week for my pension from 1912 when I passed the doctor.

In my job I met King George VI. He interviewed us at the Guildhall yard and he was a very, very nice man.

The Union

The City Corporation was a Tory body. They found out that they got on better with a trade union than with none; it was better to negotiate with the union than with Tom, Dick and Harry going for an increase in pay. And the City Corporation has never, to my knowledge, had a strike. I was in the Municipal Workers. I was branch secretary for years. We used to have our headquarters in the Nag's Head public house in Houndsditch.

I became secretary in 1918/19. I've had some decent people behind me, such as Tommy Bottley. George Lansbury and Jack Jones were interested in my Union affairs. I used to go to Fairburn Hall. I went there to a meeting, with George Lansbury. He was put in prison over giving the dustmen £4, when their real wages was 25s a week. He was bailed out by this private bloke.

I think the membership of our branch was about a third when we set it up. You used to pay 2d a week to the Union and they used to say, "Well, what are we getting out of it?". The Guildhall recognised our Union. I went to the Guildhall — I had a lumpy feeling before the Court of Common council; I shivered in my boots, I'm not ashamed to admit it. You're facing a Court of Common Councillors, and it's like a horseshoe, with the old boss, who was the Chairman, with this crest at the back of him. Years ago, you'd be frightened, 'cause you was frightened of the sack. But once the Corporation recognised the Union, we was on safe ground.

I went there. You were always interviewed by the Union bloke before you went into the Court.

"Now don't say this," he said, "and don't say that." He was the boss, no two ways about it, he was the bloody guv'nor. And I thought to myself:

"Well, I pay my bloody money to you, mate."

When I was Secretary, there was a man — he was a lavatory attendant. Name of Dwyer. He had worked on the Corporation for 51 years. You didn't retire at all — you got the sack. He was getting a bit slow, so they'd sack him. And so we've got to go before the Court of Common Council.

This bloke, he was 72, and he packed up on the Corporation when he was 70. Nothing at all. No pension, no nothing. And I said:

"Take the case of Mr Dwyer, who has been in the useful service of the City Corporation for 51 years. No pension. If I've got to pass my time on the City Corporation all those number of years, I'd sooner pass peacefully away in a lethal chamber."

"Get outside! Get outside!" The old usher came along and chucked me out. But I'd made my point. That bloke got 7s a week after that.

Then there was another case. A man was trotting his horse. Years ago, the City Corporation would not allow horses to be trotted. So when the bloke went up before Bill Heavey, our superintendent, he gave him three days suspended without pay for trotting his horse. But it was a train went over Blackfriars Arch, and frightened the horse. We took his case up to the Court of Common Council, and he got paid his three days.

People and Places

I quite remember well, when the "Thunderer" was being built at the Thames Iron Works in Canning Town, and the bow of the boat was stretching right over the roadway of what we then called "The Marsh". A friend of mine was a rivet boy, working on the "Thunderer", and he used to heat the rivets, and make them almost white hot. I can remember that boat, in the River Lea it would be, just about where the Chemical Works is at the other side of the river.

I can remember the Thames Iron Works with the West Ham Football Club in the Memorial Grounds, West Ham. You got out at West Ham Station, turned left and went over the Memorial Ground. I believe the stand is still there today.

There used to be people selling fruit in the street. This was really very, very rude: they wouldn't go to the toilet, so they'd make water in the scale as they pushed the barrow along. There used to be a lot of barrows going from along Finsbury Pavement, which is now Moorgate, down Short Street, up Moorfields, all round that block. These chaps used to have the oranges, like, done up in paper, or apples done up in paper, and they wasn't allowed to put the paper in the streets. The old ganger, he would go after the boy, or whoever it was, for not picking up the paper.

I can remember a bloke coming along selling bottles of scent, and as this bloke held out this bottle — "Here you are, put a bit of scent on you" — this bloke came along and took the bottle out of his hand and run off with it.

Then you had mock auctioneers. They had one on Aldgate. These mock auctioneers would have a box, with a lovely clock on it, and razor blades, brooches and different things like that, all scrap metal really, nothing valuable at all, but well decorated up, with colours, green and blue. These people would get a crowd round them.

Aldgate was a meat market, a Kosher meat market. I've seen the rabbi slaughter bullocks there. They used to drive the bullocks down our alley into a pair of big gates, and they used to have a kind of scaffold. On this scaffold, there'd be a crossbar, and down the

The "Thunderer"

crossbar would be two long chains with hooks on them, and as the bullock went under the scaffold they'd put this hook on a front leg, and hook on its back leg, turn a wheel, and the bullock must go over. Then the rabbi would get a square tin, and they've got to make only one cut on that bullock's throat, and if he made two cuts, that was for the English market.

Every kick that bullock done, so it would pump blood. It was a terrible death. I used to reckon it took eight minutes for the bullock to really die. Eight minutes is a long time.

Yes, and there used to be cabbies, prowling round the streets; like Hansom cabs, or four-wheelers, trouncing round the streets, trying to get people to get into hire.

I used to speak to some of the speakers on Tower Hill. I used to like to speak to Dr Soper. I believe he was a Dr of Divinity, not Medicine. he used to make me laugh, and sometimes the people would heckle him, and he would always have the right answer at the moment.

I can remember George Lansbury. The poverty was so great that — I can only have been 10 or 11 — I can remember George Lansbury and either Will Thorne or Jack Jones pulling the railings down, the wooden railings separating the pathway to the Channelsea river, to give to the people because they had no money for firing.

Oh, another thing I remember, the wooden block roads. There used to be boys and girls and men and women lining up if the London Wood Paving Company was going to dig up this wooden road, and they'd go down for the wooden blocks, because they would be all nice and tarry. The only thing is, that where the Borough Councils used to sand the streets out, the wooden blocks would be full of stones and what have you, so they had to burn them up the copper hole, because the stones would spit out.

And I can remember the clerks in Lombard Street, the financial centre of the Stock Exchange, couldn't do their work on account of the horse traffic going up Lombard Street, making a noise on the asphalt. So they pulled all the asphalt up, and the Improved Wood Paving Company put a wooden road down. I used to get a Christmas box off the asphalt people. If I saw a hole, I'd report it, and along would come the blokes and repair it.

Poverty

There was no Social Security. If you were old you had to rely on the Parish, and if the Parish did not accept you, there was the Workhouse you had to go in. And when a person was married — even if they were married for a good number of years — when they went into the Workhouse, the husband was separated from his wife. The wife went into a different building, probably a mile away from her husband. If there was anyone that died in the workhouse, the next of kin would be informed by another person who was in a grey kind of suit, or if a lady, she would have a bonnet and cape on.

At the top of Abbey Lane, there was a church. It was turned into a school, then after it was turned into a workhouse. You could see the old chaps walking about in the playground. Poverty was very bad in those days.

I can remember in Middlesex Street where the Salvation Army used to let the people in, and they used to have to lay down practically on the floor, but with wood shavings it was a lovely bed. If they got there early enough they could dry out their shirts or socks on the radiators.

Down at Billingsgate Fish Market, all the vans used to be on Eastcheap or Great Tower Street, and the barrows used to be down Billingsgate, and to get up there it was a very great hill. They put the boxes of fish on the barrows, and the Porters would say: "Up the Hill, Up the Hill", and these down and outs used to help push the barrows up the hill. They used to push these barrows and the porter used to give them either 2d or 3d, and that was how they got their 8d lodging money. Or they would hold a horse's head and get another 2d or 3d.

There was a coffee shop called Dick Fishers, which I think was in Love Lane just off Eastcheap and Billingsgate. They had a grid-iron in front of a coal fire, and they used to fry the fish — they used to pinch a little bit of fish out of the boxes. They'd have cup of tea for 1d and that was their meal. When they got to the Salvation Army they were able to buy a cup of tea either for a half-penny or a penny, and also a bun. At the back of the Salvation Army in Middlesex Street there was the ladies section.

They were in the warm, and had a bed to lay on. But those who had no money usually went along on the Embankment. What did they sleep on? The newspapers used to have what they called "Play Cards", a big bill they would hold in front of their legs, saying "A Shocking Murder in Canning Town" or whatever. They would lay on that, and if they got a lovely sheet of brown paper they would lay on that and go to sleep. The policemen never took any notice of them. They would sleep there until about 5 o'clock in the morning, and they would hurry to Billingsgate Market, which opened at 4 o'clock, to push these barrows up the hill.

The Pawnbroker

When I was 14 years of age, I can remember a man going to work, and only getting £1 per week wages to keep a family of two or three. How did they exist? The pawn shops used to be very prevalent. Over the week-end people used to look their best, but on a Monday morning their underclothing and different things used to have to go to the pawn shop. The woman used to hurry up and get the washing done, put it on the line and dry it, and send it to the pawn shop. How did it use to go? The woman had a pram, four wheels, and the pram would be loaded up full of parcels, and on each parcel was attached a piece of paper — how much to get on the parcels, and the name of the person and the contents of the parcel. When the woman got to the pawn shop, she would hand it over, and put down the money she got from the pawnbroker. The prams were very big in those days, where two children could sit either end, and a well in the middle, so you can guess the number of parcels.

My mother never had to go to the pawnshop, because my father, being in business, we were not too badly off, so my mother had no cause to go. But one day, there was a young girl who I was very friendly with, her name was Katy Williams, and she said:

"Have you ever been to a pawn shop?"

"No," I said.

"Come on, we'll go." That was the first time I saw the pawn shop in action. She went there with a parcel of under-clothing which her mother had washed out and she was asked to get 3s on the parcel. When we got there she handed the parcel over the counter, and the man said to her:

"Do you want these put in the drawer, or do you want them put on the ledge?" And she said:

"No, I want them put in the drawer." He made out three tickets for the parcel, one for him, one for the drawer and one for the person. Carbon paper was not used, but he had three pens joined together and the inkwell was like a trough, so that when he put one nib in the

"The pawn shops used to be very prevalent . . ."

trough, he put in the three. He looked at the bottom one, not the second or third one, and wrote the three tickets out all at once.

She got the three shillings less one penny for being put into the drawer. On the shelf it was mixed up with all the other clothing and exposed.

Even when I was courting, my father-in-law, who worked for the West Ham Gas Company as a labourer, was often out of work, and I can remember my wife, who was then seventeen or eighteen years old, her clothes being in the pawn shop for six shillings.

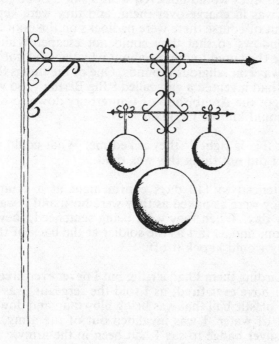

World War One

I joined up in Kitchener's Army. There were posters on all the walls saying, "Your Country Needs You", "You Are Next", and so on. It got you down, and if you had a conscience at all you would have to go and join up. I went to Stratford and I joined up, and was passed, but the doctor was a little bit doubtful about my chest. Anyway, I passed, and I was put in khaki and all that old rigmarole and was sent to Reigate. I had been in the army about two or three months when I had to have another medical examination and the doctor was rather doubtful. I had the examination at Reigate.

In the meantime, I was ordered to be in charge of two conscientious objectors who would not even wear khaki. They would not wear putties, and khaki trousers, tunic and a hat, and they walked about practically naked, they would not even wear a shirt. Good job it was summertime. I was in charge over them, and they were kept in an empty house, but of course there were padlocks on the door , and all bars on the windows so that they could not escape. While I was standing outside they used to tell me about why they did not join the army. It was always on religious grounds. One of the things they told me was that we had invented a gun called "Big Bertha". So what did they do? They got the Archbishop of Canterbury down to bless this gun so that it could kill the Germans.

"Do you think this is right?" they asked me. What could I say? I could only say I did not think this was right.

They were sentenced to 112 days confinement at a drum Court Martial, and they were as naked as they were born and it was a very cold and windy day. When they were being sentenced, they had to have their cap on, and as fast as the soldier at the back of them put on the cap, they would knock it off.

Whilst I was guarding them I had a rifle, but I never ever fired a shot. The only shot I have ever fired, as I told the sergeant, was down a fairground at a plastic ball that was being blown up and down at the end of a squirt of water. I was invalided out of the army, given a , pension and a silver badge to say I had been in the army.

One night at around 7 pm, I was going to meet my young lady who was working at Tillet's Laundry at the Romford Road. I was going from Canning Town to Stratford, and as I got to the Lord Goff, West Ham, there was a terrible explosion and I jumped off the tram. There was a lot of people that got killed. The explosion was at Brunner Mond, and as my mother lived in Canning Town, I went to see if she was alright. I went back home and found my mother OK, but shocked; and I got on the tram again and went to see my future mother-in-law and she was OK. By the time I got there my young lady was home from work. I shall always remember that explosion.

Another thing I always remember, and that was the Zeppelin. I can see it now, catching alight over Potters Bar. From where I was standing the flames were absolutely terrific. I thought the crew of the Zeppelin all perished.

We never had radio nor television, and people had to make their own amusements. We read newspapers for one halfpenny. there was the Evening News, the Star and Standard and the Daily Herald. We got the newspaper, and it told us that an aeroplane went over the top of the Zeppelin, bombed it, and set it on fire.

There was a firm in West Ham named the Leathercloth, and my mother-in-law worked there making bandoliers for the soldiers. Women came into their own absolutely, working at all kinds of things, on the buses and the trams and different things, munitions as well. And I remember there was a man that worked in the TNT in Woolwich Arsenal, and his face, hands and clothing was all yellow with this TNT.

Amusements

Seeing that we had no radio or television, people had to make their own amusements. The street organ came along. Unemployment was very, very bad; you would see on the side of the organ — "Unemployed". The people used to sing:

> "We've got no work to do,
> We've got no work to do,
> We're out of work,
> We're out of work,
> And we've got no work to do."

They used to have a bowler hat or a trilby on the front of the organ. As the man used to turn the handle, people used to put a half-penny or one penny in — whatever they could afford. The people would say on the organ: "We are unemployed, we've got 4, 5 or so many children to keep". They went down the street, and the organ grinder would grind his old organ, the young girls and people would sing the songs of the organ, and dance round it, and if it was summertime people would sit outside drinking a cup of tea and gossiping. The Salvation Army lads and lassies, they used to be singing hymns and that — they were very good indeed. People used to throw their half-pennies or pennies in the circle.

My first gramophone I bought for my mother because she could sing a lovely song. My father could also sing. I remember it had a blessed great horn on this gramophone, and the records were round, like cylinders. You had to put the needle in properly otherwise it would not play at all. It was clockwork, and had to be wound by handle.

Where I took Blind Ben about, he played a portable harmonium. I naturally watched where his fingers went. There was a pawn shop in Bow which had a portable harmonium for sale, and it was £2. My brother-in-law bought it for me but I paid him back. I played this portable harmonium, and my mother would sing. I used to go out and buy a linnet for 3d, and the more my mother sang, and the more I played, the more the bird would sing. And a bullfinch I bought for 6d — it had a little barrow, and pulled it up on a piece of string by his beak to catch the seed, and the same thing when I had a little pail, and he would pull the pail up with the string.

"They used to have opera up the Borough Theatre in Stratford"

Very often we would go out on a Saturday night. I'm not a beer drinker, but I'm a port wine drinker, and my job took me down into wine vaults, and they used to give me a drink down there. So my wife said to me one day, before we were married:

"I don't know, you keep on talking about Dirty Dick's, Dirty Dick's, Dirty Dick's — I've never been down there." I said:

"Right, we'll go down there." So I met her one Saturday night around six o'clock. The horse buses were running. So I said to her:

"What are you going to have when you get down there?" She said:

"I'll have what you have, like, have a drop of port wine." So I said "Alright."

You could go down there, and you could buy a glass of port wine for tuppence. I had a glass, she had a glass, and I said:

"Have another one?"

"No, I don't want another one."

I had one. As we came up the stairs of Dirty Dick's, she kind of stumbled, so I said:

"'Ere, come on, what's the matter with you?"

"I don't half feel funny," she said, "I feel as though I'm going to fall down." Before I could catch hold of her arm, she bashed into this upright iron standard. In those days, women wore hats with a wide rim on the hat. Of course, it knocked it for six. So, we walked down Houndsditch to the bus stop at Aldgate. Oh, everybody was looking at me, you know, so we gets on this horse bus, gets inside, and the old conductor looks at me, and he looked at her; and as she sat on the seat, the rim of her hat caught on the glass on the back, and tipped the front of her blooming hat up. And everybody who was getting on the bus was saying:

"Look, the little monkey, he's got her drunk."

When we got home, her mother crumped me. Cor, we never went out no more that evening! It could not have been half past seven. We used to stay out till about twelve, half past twelve.

I went in for a competition, which I failed, for playing the piano. I don't play by music, I only play by ear, but if you want to get up and give a song, or anything like that . . . I played in pubs.

I was no beer drinker. I don't drink hardly any spirits. The only thing I might have is a bit of rum and milk, and my old boy used to have that. My father used to like his rum and milk.

Before the war, you used to have public house football teams. When my father used to have his ponies or donkeys on the Shute, as we called it, the Arrow used to play there, the Arrow public house in High Street, Stratford. You got better football then than what you do today. I've only been to two or three football matches. I've got no interest. But if you was to say there was a car rally, or car racing, I'd go and see that. Even today I'm interested in cars. For instance, if my daughter's car is up the creek, I'll have a bash.

My mother, she used to like opera. They used to have opera up the Borough Theatre, in Stratford. That Mr Parker used to take my mother, because my father was so busy with his business, like, ponies and donkeys. He hadn't got no time to go to operas or anything, and besides, he wasn't that way inclined.

My wife and I were rare ones for going up the Stratford Empire, first house, and going up to the Borough, or the Theatre Royal, up in Angel Lane.

Round about 1912, I was courting and I took my young lady to the Chant Square Picture Palace where they were showing silent pictures of Charlie Chaplin. To go to the pictures it was only 3d and you got a back seat. Where you paid 1d you sat on forms, but if you paid 3d you sat on a plush seat. Then again we would go to the Stratford Empire, and we would see different turns there; paid 6d to go in and there was always a man with a large basket and for 1d he would sell a bag of peanuts. By the time you lined up and you went into the Empire you would be treading on peanut shells.

The Circus

I must tell you — there was another thing I remember as a boy. There was a circus in High Street Stratford. My mother sent me out to get 1 lb of butter, and I saw these lovely caravans. There was a large caravan pulled by four or six horses, but they could not pull this long caravan up the hill. I watched them struggling, and they gave up. All of a sudden, I noticed a coloured man come along with an elephant, and the elephant got its shoulder alongside this caravan and pushed it up the hill.

There was a lot of funfairs you could go to. There used to be a boxing booth down Stratford, and there would be two or three men get on to the platform outside the tent and take on all comers. They would throw out a pair of gloves to the man who was going to fight three rounds of boxing. A pal of mine and me, who used to draw water out of the pond to drive the engines for the roundabout, and got in with this boxing booth, we heard him say:

"Yes, I'll have a go with you."

"Alright, come on, you come in then." But as he got the gloves on and went inside, we heard him say:

"Now look, don't hit too hard, just make a show, that's all." And of course the two men would get in the ring and have a go and no-one would win as it was arranged.

Cars

I had an early car — I bought a Ford. I paid ten quid for it. It had a box body to enable me to take different things from home to the ground that I bought at Rainham. This was about 1925; and coming home one day, it was pouring with rain and I broke down. It was magneto driven — not coil ignition — and no water should get on the points of the magneto. I was wearing a cap, and so that the water would not get on the magneto, I put my cap over it. I didn't know what was happening. A man came along in a big four-ton lorry, who lived at Rainham:

"I can do that for you," he said, "But I'll have to tow you back to Rainham." So he towed us back, my wife and me.

"I can't do it now," he said, "but I'll do it in the morning." The job he done on that car, it took him about five minutes. He took the first spark plug out of the socket, he turned the magneto round to the number 1 firing point and he put the plug back and the car started as though nothing has happened to it! I had that Ford and it did a lot of work for me, but then again I could not go too far with it. So I bought another one, a Panhard Levass — it was supposed to be a French Rolls Royce. I bought that for £40. That was coil ignition and we went all over the place with it. One of the places we went to was Winchester and that was where I saw a bird catcher catching different wild birds such as greenfinches, chaffinches and linnets and what have you. They caught the birds in a little net, and he would be under a hedge, and then pulled the string so that the two halves of the net came down.

The Panhard was a very, very, very good car. I used to run backwards and forwards to me piece of ground at Rainham and fetch back what my wife had grown, such as potatoes. You could go and buy potatoes for 4 lb a penny.

Married life

We had three days' holiday when I was a boy, but that didn't come until about three years after I'd started at the City of London. When I was storekeeping, I got a week's holiday. We went down to Southend. It was half a crown there and back. We went to Hartington Street. Lockhart's coffee shop was on the corner. We lodged with a woman named Mrs. Bracket. I always remember that; brackets is what you put on the walls. Stout old girl she was.

We had a week down there. Not many people had holidays — they couldn't afford them. I took my wife down there — we were single then. I always remember the old girl, she stood there: I couldn't see how she could get in the door.

"Ah," she said, "you're the two. You're single."

"Yes," my wife said.

"And no walking in your sleep, neither. You mind how you go." She gave me her bloody lip, honestly, this woman. "No walking in your sleep." 'Course, we had separate rooms.

Anyway, I got married in 1917 by special licence, and we lived at number 8, Middle Road, for about 6 years.

I went home one day, and I looked at the rent book, I had a good job, and I wasn't like, flush with money, but we had enough to live on, and more besides with it. I looked, and I saw 6s 6d, 6s 6d, 6s 6d, all the way down this bloody rent book. So I said to my wife:

"What about us buying a place?"

And I went to my brother-in-law.

My brother-in-law and my sister were business people. He worked part time for the Lea Iron Foundry, and he had a contract there to cart all the valuable iron and cast iron, gates and what have you for the Foundry. Before he died in 1917, my father was living with my brother, my sister and my brother-in-law. He'd already retired, sold up.

"'Ere, I'd like to buy a place," I said to my brother-in-law.

"Yes, alright," he said. "I'll tell you what we'll do." So my wife, and me and him, we went to Bostocks in Green Steet, near Upton Park Station. My brother-in-law gave me all this gen about how to look at property. So we saw this house, 55 Kingsland Road.

"That's nice," I said to her, but there was people in it. "Let's have a look in and see what these people have got to say." So we went in.

"Oh yes," they said, "We've got to get out if anybody buys it, because it's decontrolled. So it don't make any difference, if you want to buy. But I wouldn't buy it, the bloody rotten hole." Honestly! So I said to my wife:

"What do you think?"

"I like the street," she said — so I said:

"What about the house, do you like the house".

So we went back to old Bostocks. It was advertised for £400. My brother-in-law said to me:

"Don't ever give what they ask. You go down to a price, you can always come up, but you can't come down again." So I went back to old Bostock.

"That house in Kingsland Road," I said.

They were wanting to sell houses those days: there wasn't many houses for sale, it was all to let.

"Oh yes." he said, "£400".

"No, I wouldn't pay £400," I said, "I'll tell you what, I'll give you £350 for it, but make it snappy, 'cause I got another two to look at." I hadn't, but that's what I said.

"Oh," he said, "You're a hard man. Charlie!" he said, "Fetch in a coffee." So Charlie brought in three cups of coffee.

"We went down to Southend"

There's old Bostock, me and my wife, we're all haggling over the price. But he did come down to £350. I don't know what my daughter got when she sold it, but of course I'd greatly improved it. I'm a little bit of a builder myself. I knocked the wall down and made a through lounge.

I moved there, 55 Kingsland Road, Plaistow, about 1929; two bedrooms up and two rooms down, with a kitchen and a nice garden. I got the money from a Solicitor — he still practices in East Ham. My wife went to work at a laundry to help me pay back the £350. Directly I paid up the house, I asked my wife to leave off work.

Trams

I can remember when the trams were pulled along by two horses. When it got to its destination, from Stratford to Bow Bridge, they put the horses on the other side of the tram — and bob's your uncle, in reverse. The trams at night time would all be off the road. There were no covered trams, not then.

My cousins drove the horse tram from Stratford to Bow Bridge. Later, several boroughs, Poplar, Bow, Stepney, agreed to the West Ham Borough running their trams to Aldgate. I can remember when — I think it was Roosevelt — used to give every horse bus driver a brace of pheasants, and you'd see them alongside the dickie.

Then came the electric trams. They'd have this thing, with a big handle and two prongs, and it would already be on the line, but they'd have to push it underneath the tram to get the electricity. And the seats on top of the trams were all open. The back of the seats you could move — if you were going to Aldgate, you would face going to Aldgate; turn the back of the seat back again and you would face Stratford. At the back of the seats there was a tarpaulin cover, so when it rained you would not get wet if you got right under the tarpaulins. There was the overhead wire system which went from Bow Bridge or the Iron Bridge eastwards; when you went westwards you had the three track system, where they got in the power from the middle line.

In the 1930s we got the trolley buses. There were overhead wires. The only benefit was that they could get on the bus from the kerb; a person walked to the middle of the road to get on a tram. After that you got the petrol buses, which were a boon.

Women

You know, the woman, in my opinion, had a very bad life years ago. They might go out office cleaning in the morning, getting up at 5 o'clock. The housekeeper of the block would see that they were there, and they had to be out of the offices at 8 o'clock. The fare from Stratford to Aldgate was 1d there and 1d back. These women, they didn't earn very much money but they were always a very happy bunch of people.

Then it would be 8.45 to 9.00 am, and they would get the kids off to school; then have a wash and what have you: and after that, do their washing and their housework. I think they had a very bad life, whereas the man, he couldn't help it. I can remember when men were leaning up against public houses because they couldn't get any work; they would get fed up with nothing to do. 1926, you had the General Strike.

What would washing day be like?

The woman would have to light the copper, and very often the fire would go out. Then she would get a sack and try to beat the copper hole where the fire was, to make the coal and wood catch alight. After getting the water boiling in the copper, she would get the stick and put the clothes in a bath and rub the clothes on the washing board. Then she would get the wringer and put the clothes through. After the washing was partly dry she would do the ironing on the table.

There were no carpets hardly in those days, and if you had lino you were very, very well off. The women would sweep the floor, and get the hot water from the copper where the washing was done and scrub the ordinary boards on the floor. With the fireplace you had the hearth to keep nice and white. The copper would have to be cleaned out, and the ashes from the fire.

Regarding the cooking, she didn't do much. Meat was very cheap, vegetables were almost thrown at you. Potatoes 4 lb for 2d for the best ones; greens as well; you could buy cheaply. You had to live cheaply, because the man didn't earn very much money. If he earned 30s a week, that was a lot.

We had the open fire grate in the best room, and if you didn't have much money, it never hardly got lit. The main one was the kitchen, it had to be black-leaded and polished and God knows what. You did all the cooking by the oven; there was no gas cookery then, unless you were very well off.

The Fly House

You know the Fly House? You go along Bridge Road, and you go over Barking Station — they used to have a level crossing — and there's a pub, on the corner. I don't know what the name of it is. Look at the top, you'll see a steeple up there and it's got a fly on top of it. There was farms all around there when I was twelve, and my Uncle Jimmy and my Aunt Ellen used to farm there, and there was only two houses.

Years ago, time was nothing. We didn't use to rush years ago. The farm labourers used to have a waggon with two horses pulling it — the horses wouldn't be side by side, one would be ahead of the other in the shafts. For reins they had a long rope, and they'd have what they called a ladder. It'd be about 2 feet wide coming down from the van over the horses' backs. You wouldn't have a dickie or anything like that for the driver to sit in — the old driver used to lay down on this ladder and go to sleep. They had the old rope hanging down from the piece of lattice work at the back, where all the other produce was in the waggon. It'd have say, cabbages or bags of potatoes, cauliflowers and what have you, taking it to Spitalfields Market or Covent Garden. The pubs would close at about 11 o'clock. They used to start away. The horses knew where to go, they didn't want no driving, they'd go to Spitalfields Market or Covent Garden as easy as wink. Then, the coppers would come along:

"Oi! Come on — wake up!" and they'd wake up.

This man, it was supposed to be my cousin, but I don't think it was any relation, he was a carter. He told me the reason why it was called the Fly House. Of a night-time, they used to take this produce to Covent Garden. Coming back they'd load up with a load of horse manure, and in the hot weather the flies would all be on this hot dung, and the old carter used to stop there for a drink in the morning (it used to be open all day) and all the flies used to go in the pub.

World War II

Of course, me knowing a bit about cars — cars really wasn't so prominent — when I joined the ARP in 1939 I was on the Ambulance. I saw it right through until 1945. I had to have a road test. You can guess I saw some terrible sights. One thing I will always remember was that I tried to resuscitate a Jewish gentleman, with his wife. He was lying on the kerb and saying:

"It's my breath, it's my breath." He said this many times, hitting his chest all the time. I laid the man down and gave him the kiss of life. Eventually, unfortunately, he died. His wife gave me a watch.

I said to my wife:

"Well, look, it's like this. I am going to join the ARP, so therefore the house will be empty." So I asked her if she would like to be evacuated. Everyone was going. So I sent my wife and children, two girls, to Spelsbury in Oxford. My wife worked on the farm whilst she was down there. She made hay. I used to go down there to see them about once in every nine or ten weeks.

I saw my daughter off from school on the morning that they were going to be evacuated. I well remember that, because I really got told off by the teacher — I should not have gone. My daughter was happy, with her other little playmates, but when she saw me, naturally enough she wanted to come home. The coach was supposed to be at New City Road School by 9 o'clock. I went there with them to see my wife and youngest daughter off, but the coach didn't arrive until round about 11 o'clock, when I had to get ready for work. That was the Saturday.

When the furniture went down there on account of the bombing, I let the house to a person for 12s 6d per week rent.

I was in the Guildhall fire, and when I went down to see my wife about 5 or 6 weeks after the fire, she told me that she could see the fire reflection in the sky when the London Docks were burning. I didn't know at the time, but I rescued the Town Clerk's wig and gown. We tried to rescue some books that were in the iron safe and the building was very hot. The door slammed as the four of us went in, and what with the heat, and the expansion of the iron doors, we had a hard job to get out. We got the books out alright, and we took them to Maidenhead, to a place that was owned by the Corporation.

I can remember . . .

I can remember when we never had gas lamps in the streets. We had oil lamps, and a bloke used to come round with a big tank on a pair of wheels and two legs to lodge them on. You had an iron bar across the post near the lamp. Kids used to throw a rope over that bar and make a swing of it. He'd go up — he used to put his ladder up on the bar.

I can remember when gas first came into the lamps in the streets. They had a nipple with a snick in the top, and that's where you had the jet. I can remember the veritous mantles, then you had the upright mantles. The blokes used to have these mantles in a kind of box. You had to be careful; they was made of asbestos I believe, and they was very fragile — you only had to touch them, and they'd go to bits.

I can remember Rainham when there were no street lights there. I can remember Basildon when there was no water there. I bought a piece of ground at Rainham about 1927. It was 35' frontage, 200' deep. It had a ditch running along it, and Churchill's, the timber merchants, was up the side.

Where they dug the Hollow Pond in Wanstead; where they got the water was supposed to be an artesian well. They had one in Stoney Lane. Because in some parts of the City, a lot of the parts where people used to live, they had no water laid on. I can remember that in 1914/15, where in Providence Place they had no water laid on. I can remember bits of things. It's built up so much today. I went up the City, and it's all altered up there — I wouldn't know it. Don't think I'd like to work up there now.

Typical shop in Newham in the 1900's

A family shop early in 1900's

OTHER PARENTS' CENTRE PUBLICATIONS

The London Blitz — A Fireman's Tale by C. Demarne, OBE

£1.80

An East London Picture Book 82 b/w photos 1860-1920

£1.80